DREAMY CICADA

MAKENA M MUTUA

Copyright © 2012 Maxadria Makena

Cover design by @affectreflect@gmail.com

Redesigned by: Michael Mutua

ISBN: 9789966804389
ISBN-13: 978-9966-804-38-9

<u>DEDICATION</u>

This book is for **YOU**

LET'S BEGIN

Have loved the bumps of this wonderful journey,
writing as much as I could drink and we both know
one can never get enough, I
hope you like the bumps as much I do, I
hope you learn to laugh while you ache, I hope you love
so your bones can dance upon these soft
stories.

everyone who truly loved, believed, and shared my stories
thank you for getting me here, you are part of the musing

CARRY ME WITH YOU

If my scars will never heal, paint them,
If my tears will never cease drown In them,
And if my heart is burdened carry it with you,
And beloved if am this heavy like they say,
Rest upon the mountains, feast upon the beasty of hearts,
Stay with me long enough, on storms written my name,
On nights terrifying as death,
On roads longer than eternity,
Darling carry me with you until the end of days,
Carry me with you till I can smile again,
Carry me with you for there will be good days,
Just carry me with you.

THE SUN STILL RISES!

The sun still rises
 gracefully like a heart wasn't broken
yesterday!
forces itself in your room
without a knock!
Even thou you don't need the nagging
How is it this eager to rise again…
It burns, oh it burns all your dreams,
The sun still rises,
dances with the clouds like you need the show!
ending, leaving and looking beautiful,
then you start to like its company, on evening
the way it turns and cools, you clasp its setting,
you want it to stay,
but it doesn't stop, it only rises…
the sun still rises and leaves all the same!
The sun still rises and leaves again,
to give you love, to leave. To come again…
and again.

THE ART OF THE HURT
Judge my pain
beg me to forget
say that it's not worth
then offer me love
 serve it gently and plain,
without wounds
I will take it quick (oh the way it burns),
then leave so someone else can do
the same,
it's a circle which never ends.

EVERYTHING GOES TO DUST

You are as beautiful as you think,
The same skin you ran your fingers through
And felt alive, will shrink and wrinkle
Over an overlapped time, the same tongue you rolled
Slower with lies and faster with truths
Will tremble and fall inside of your chin,
The eyes which showed off your heart
Will not tell the color of the skies!
The same lips which kissed
Rights and wrongs will hug by your mouth,
Tired and heavy!
The ears which eavesdropped on love
Will lie dead by the side of your head!
I hope then you will have,
Broken enough hearts, lived all dreams,
And became everything you wished.

ALL MY UNREPLIED EMAILS

The last time I wrote to you I wrote in tears
you will never understand,
this world has shocked me too
since I emailed, you couldn't see the stains of my
tears, how I ran out of ink, the spots of dirt upon
my nostalgic letters,
maybe then you would have replied,
and in turn I would see the rich colors of
your pen, your handwriting am sure people like
you hardly cry, then I would weep again in joy staining
your countries neat postcards.

UNENDING TEARS

I knew there were no tears left after you!
no more pain
here I am thinking of the ocean inside of me
because your story keeps getting better
you are with her
and am with tears
when you begin I cry.

WHAT'S YOURS IS MINE

Stay with me,
one more minute
then you can leave,
without your heart!
Have never stolen anything
but the way yours is put out in the open like
that, I will snatch it! Oh lord how I want to!
now Go, leave,
then you shall return
when you learn that something is missing,
you will look for me,
you will ask for something in return,
I will give you what's yours
and it will be mine, it will never be the same.

PRIORITIES

He never
loved
me and that
shattered my heart, but oh
how I want this pain to sit still
so I can breathe.

DEMON DRESSED LIKE AN ANGEL

Have known rain
for it's cleansing of this earth
have known you
for the loving, for the pain
for the scars,
And have wished you could
be anything like it,
even after a long time of
summer,
that….when you come again
I should be overwhelmed,
I should dance and wet myself,
but you my dear,
have made me afraid!
of anything like you,
every demon dressed like an angel.

RIGHT

We love the right people for the right
reasons, it might seem like the wrong time!
Or the wrong place, but when we let love,
There's never the right place,
There's never the right reason,
There's never the right person,
There's never the right time,
There's only you and them,
And a couple of forever's aligned
neatly to get lost in.

THE MISSING PIECES OF MY HEART

He gave me a string to tie on the wall
of my heart
back then love was playful and young
so he climbed on
one day while we rested
he climbed down
using the same string
and then love became
a bit sour and tearful,
and that's how I lost some pieces
of my heart,
I don't know whether
they still hang by the string or they fell
on his jacket!
 he has never climbed back on ever,
and without those pieces I can never climb down
am not strong enough.

PREACHING WHISKEY

Have loved enough to know what love is
and what love is not, but when it comes
to you am the fool! Spilling water
and preaching whiskey to
my aching heart.

DYING FOR YOU

I will never forget your name
or how well you breathe,
but my love you love too little
and I do not blame you,
 I was meant to drown so you can
 breathe that way,
I was meant to die so you can leave.

A LOVE NOTE

Leave me a note, on top of my words,
which say I love you sometimes,
leave me a note, on an empty bottle,
corked tightly to sail through the Indian Ocean
leave me a note, on the feet of an Asian hawk,
the fastest one, I love to read every dawn,
leave me a note, around my heart,
the most wounded bottom,
Where our love was born.

OUT WITH MY HEART

My heart won't do this with me,
I want to dive in and drown in something new,
I want to die at the bottom of the sea,
not here, not like this,
my heart won't do this with me,
 it won't forget it won't be fooled
no matter how much
 I take it there
where my skin was hanged to dry
where nails with the scent of its blood scatter
'These are the nails which were driven through you"

my heart won't do this with me
It will never elope, or beat for another,
like I want.

DECEIT

Feed me lies and I will eat
have been hungry
have sought to be fed
but be careful
I bite
and your lies will bleed truths
before I swallow.

BELONGING WITH STARS

I was always seduced by boys who wore hats,
Setting my tongue on the phrase
"All men are the same"
but men rarely wear hats and talk too little
yet feel so much,
you only know how they feel when they hold
you strongly against themselves,
 they only need the moon,
the same way they fetch stars just
 to make you moan! The same way their eyes
look into yours while you burn just for them,
I can no longer contain
young boys who need praise, and talk a lot yet feel nothing,
I am a woman now, a star woman.

LOVE WITHOUT THEM

When love finally finds you,
And you can't decide…
whether their presence and absence
overwhelms you,
or if the distance is just the space
between l and e or flights away,
whether their future or now would be
forever, or whether
you would rather die for them,
do not run…
love is here with you
without them.

FALLING INTO THE FIRE

Would you have thought
that one person could make
you feel so much,
they say you cannot warm
yourself around fire for too long
without falling into it, out of sleep and comfort,
you fell in too deep,
now it's all cold and all your scars show.

GENTLE

We blame our hearts
for what we cannot forget
or what we regret,
forgetting that
the heart, mind, spirit and body
are a team
just that each has its own way
of erasing what the other
can no longer contain
let's be gentle with them
for they are not gentle to each other.

THE UNIVERSE AND YOU

I was trapped inside of your words
declining myself the universe
these days am trapped in the
universe with your words everyday
playing in the background
but I can never have you.

GRACEFULLY

Un-love me,
Un-know me,

You have told me all this
Without letting out a sound!
now
I will un-love you,
I will UN-know you,
gracefully.

THE TYPE

He was a lot like coffee
most times in the morning
bad times and winter everyday
though he tasted like my
favorite chocolate,
he rarely came home!
and when he did it was the black
 sugarless type
bitter, comforting and hot.

LOVE IS NOW

It will always feel like love
the beautiful poems…
the slow halloos…
the swift kisses….
the soft slides through our slippery palms…
the quick conversations…
the irrational tingling's of the stomach…
the fast heartbeats…
the sweet short stories…
the goofy photographs…
but it wasn't ….
love is now …
now that you are not here.

SAVAGE

I'll rip you open when I see you!
your eyes,
your heart,
your skin,
gently without breaking,
then I will feed with my eyes closed
so I wouldn't have to look into yours ever again…
I will rip you off and leave you for the vultures
am sure they will enjoy
savaging your bones after me,
See we are not that different after all.

POEMS FOR YOU

In the end words slide to your favor,
the way you cry,
the way you laugh,
the way you love,
the way you leave,
so many poems began like different kind
of stories, but ended up here,
maybe you are more beautiful than you thought,
maybe this is why we write,
so we can slip and tell about you.

THE GRAVEYARD

And in the grave where I lay,
among strangers
harvesting tears and watching my
flowers wither, words said became so true,
I was truly missed, and some have
wished upon my grave for me to wake
again, some curse " damnit why
did you have to go"
and though my bones are old
I can afford a laugh, the world felt
so lonely! And now these words
down with me, how rich it is, how lonely it isn't,
voices upon voices, words upon words.

REPLAY

I would wish to stick a knife through his
chest and pull out his heart, just like he did to mine
just like he does just that he uses knives
made of L's and O's
and all the sweet words of the alphabets
 but am nothing like him I would go to the same
spot he loved me, the same spot he left me,
just to replay what he can never feel,
pain for me, anger for me,
love for me and loss for me,
I replay feelings of two people in one heart!

HUM ALONG

I hum along, when I think of you,
as a heartbeat
felt along my veins, so is my life,
as you dance in my eyes,
It's breathless and full. I dream along,
when you hold my hand,
gentle as the breeze I see you
being every part of me
 I live along because of the breaths
you take away, caressing me by the spine,
leaving me defenseless,
how can I ever live without you?
 I hold along
all the beauty you bring, never drift away my love,
you are all I will ever want, this lifetime and any other.

A STRANGER IN MY SMALL TOWN

He speaks like he's from the colonies
in the coffee shop, and everyone listens closely,
this dinner shop is that small,
no space to breathe your air and they say
one can hear your thoughts if you stay long enough!
But it's the favorite spot for free spirits and story tellers,
I order my coffee and sit by, now that there's a stranger in town,
I too crave to get something out of him,
his stories are wise and slow, when his eyes meet mine, he pauses,
and this wanderer is shaken, and that intrigues,
our small town is not safe for such admirations,
I look away and go on sipping bit by bit,
late in the dark, I catch him alone,
"I need a story of my own too" I say,
he rants throwing his thin hands on the
brightest stars, so captivating…
Then he places beads from seven countries on my palms
each with its tale and adventure,
oh those hands are so warm! We hold for much longer,
I welcome him in this town, we sit by a fire,
I tell him of our tradition and ,I insist he shut his eyes,
I sure bluff to admire his skin without his beautiful
big judging eyes, he tells me about the places he has been,
the beautiful women and the valleys,
and from his eyes, his hair and all of him are poems I recite,
 now he has to go,
"Do you do this to women in every small town you go" I ask
he kisses my arm and takes a picture of me,
our chief says that, my heart will forever hunger,
oh this town and its gossip.

IF ONLY I COULD DRAW

If I knew how to draw, I would draw my past naked,
I would clown it with wings and paint it black,
It would be easy then, I would blow it away and it would fly,
and a naked black past would fly away,
If I knew how to draw I would draw three hearts!
I would paint them red, black and white!
I would love without abhorring with the red heart!
I would hate with an ache with the black heart!
I would make interminable peace with the white heart!
and then It would be a massive!
If I knew how to draw I would draw a friend,
I would paint all colors, and then he would stay forever,
I would lean on him I would spend the rest of my days with him,
I would grow old by his side I would love with him,
I would cry with him, he would listen to me, the friend
of mine I made only true to me
but then I don't know how to draw.

LATERN

I was possessed by drifting into sleep
  thinking of you,
sometimes you would hold me and wrestle me to bed,
that passion terrified me,
at 2 am sunny dusty and busy
you crossed my mind,
I finally lit a lantern so I wouldn't sleep,
I would put it off in the morning
Just to chase the figures,
but no matter how bright it shone all through the night,
darkness reigned for the ache of your absence,
and my lantern is the reminder that
on some nights I have to chase you.

DREAMS AND THEIR DEATHS

I know you hold her and promise her
forever's the same way I held you and promised you the same,
I know you love her the same way I loved you
or even more for then it feels right,
I know you would give the world for her to be happy,
the same way I would give the world to see you smile,
oh and the poetries! do you slip small notes
under her pillow while she sleeps?
Is she your new found muse?
The same way I Imagined us exchanging
beautiful poems across seas,
she touches you on most nights, you watch stars together,
you chase dawns hands locked,
you have the same dreams, just almost, she takes photographs,
but most of yours are hers,
you see her every day, you go with her everywhere,
both of you are living my dream, and that's okay,
 you found her and I lost you,
hope she never has to leave like you left,
hope you never hurt like I do,
it's a dream of mine that you will never have to lie in bed like this
and dream of her like I dream of you.

LET ME LOVE YOU

Let me love you,
when you can see no more,
let me love you,
when you can't wake,
let me love you,
when the earth doesn't spin,
let me love you,
when you cannot understand,
let me love you,
when you do not know,
let me love you,
when you cannot dream,
let me love you,
when there's no more peace,
 for my Love what's the use of love
when you can see am not right for you,
when you can wake and leave me by myself,
when the world spins and you go a million
 miles away from me,
when you can understand why I love you so much
when you know my weakness and spots
when you can dream of another
when peace drives you to tranquil far from here
for then you can never love me back.

CHURCH GOERS

The Vickers preached with such wisdom and glory
the words flapped the windows open, and closed the doors,
but hearts lay dead between their chests,
heads nodding, mouths uttering "Amen, Amen…in unison,
eyes lied every chance they got, wide awake
minds were in the midst of sways and chaos,
the vicars handkerchief couldn't wipe these sweats no more,
and when he shrubs, the church falls with laughter,
there is some little life now but not when he told
of adultery the ten commandments and love,
It's time to for sacrament and they clean the glasses so well
and prepare the table,
In the end the vicars shrub is stuck to the
 heart and mouths than the word of that day.

SADNESS

Sadness came home again,
Crawled on my bed before me,
Waved a hand, and indication that it was tired,
It wore my eyes,
Had my cheeks,
Breathed my air,
Put on my night sandals,
And it was beautiful,
As it slept,
As I wailed the night away,
Sadness came home again.

LOVE'S NOT SAFE

Am not lucky, I know,
for when love falls
It's on the other side of town
and when it's calm I watch from my window
some love doves flying,
above and below,
others praising
theirs and another,
and when it's full of abyss
there's a distress call
from the towns chapel
Oh come and see,
she's torn,
Oh come and see
she's dead,
Oh come and see
she's nothing
the OH's go on and on
till Christmas
and when its new year there's a resolution
with less OH's and love torrents
am not lucky I know
and love isn't either, I will watch from here
till its safe to play in the sun, without the smell of love!

COME WITH ME

Come with me,
let's catch the next flight,
let's forget the world,
and the scars come with me,
with every piece of yourself,
tell me how you like your coffee,
your favorite channel,
Come with me, to a point of no return,
not here my love, away before the last fall
after our merry kisses,
Come with me,
let's dance to this song we write everyday
let's serenade these birds,
whispering close to our souls,
Come with me,
where souls like our own, do not know goodbyes
where souls like our own
define love with knotted threads
without their end or the beginning.

WITHOUT

He's looking for something of his
he lost,
but first he finds his ego
and picks it,
then he forgets,
he wants something of his
he can't live without
but first he furnishes his pride
then he is fine.
there's something of his out there,
broken and full of regrets,
but when he gets there,
something important comes up
he goes back again to live without.

THE DEATH OF OUR LOVE

If our love ever dies,
let it die with our names
and the songs we used to sing,
while we loved
if our love ever dies
let it die with our shame
and the caresses we awakened
while we loved If our love ever dies
let it die with our memories
and all the places we ever travelled
while we loved
If our love ever dies, let it die with us!
If our love dies Like it did
let us crown it
with silence, pride and puzzles.

BE…

Be beautiful girl,
Like the lilies,
And like yourself too,
Be beautiful girl,
So they wish to lay with you,
But you girl
Do not wish to lay with them,
Be beautiful girl
Even in your beast days,
Jump and dance a little
Be beautiful girl,
Be fierce,
Just be beautiful girl,
Just be you.

HOME

"This our way home" they say
but I do not stagger! I know too well
where my home is
these lights will lead me there I know,

But home is a familiar place
with fine decors and laughter sometimes they tell me,
"You are not yet home!"
But am there making burnt cookies
peeking in the television my favorite show is on
 I know the place well
few corners from main town
fine gate and dogs a living room, a bedroom
a lobby and the kitchen
they say that's what I tell myself that I do
not know a thing about my home
these voices in my head
sound deceitful .

WHEN HE TALKS ABOUT HER

You should hear him talk about her,
the soft buzz in her voice
which wakes him in the morning,
her eyes the way they open and close
and he would say, her soul opens before me
and I can't help it, the way she cries
and he can hear himself breaking,
and her scars... He has mastered each one
of them like they slipped
from childhood holding hands! the way she speaks its
like she builds a new whole
place for him to live in, her laughter is like a
new breath except that she grants it to him
split like wrapped Christmas gifts just beneath his heart!
Then he sighs heavily under these stars
and smiles, "If heavens would allow me to reach the stars
I would give her some of them
just like she gives me my
life like it were fetched from
the skies"

MASQUARADES

I tip toe in the dark
afraid that love will catch me
at the middle but I make it
to the other room,
I pull the masquerades from
 the closet
and love joins me later in the night
we sit comfortably
sharing ideas, wine and
cigars then we fall asleep
and by morning he's gone
I slip the disguise right
back to the closet,
we have been doing this for years,
on different spots,
none of us knows how the other looks like,
none of us knows where we are from!

SAD STORIES

The most saddest stories are
those I think of at 3am
and I never get to write on a piece of paper
because my eyes are full of
tears!!
So when it's morning
and the dawn has whispered
it's halloos
and kissed away some sadness,
I drown in the madness
of the day, and end up
narrating about the curves
around the moon and the
cold, right before the coffee.

SOME 3AMS

You turned my mornings into
  Looking by the first light,
  A cup of coffee by or the camera
I capture that lonely rising sun
And the streaks remind me of you
Then a couple of poems
As I sip.
My nights are trapped
In 3am form where you kinder love
Making me ask myself things and make wishes
Then my favorite songs Play much slower
And I do not know whether you
Made my life better or worse
There's so much now than there was before.

ONE BEAUTIFUL LIE

You are one beautiful lie,
Covered with smoked truths
And uncertain sweet phrases
You are one beautiful lie
Dressed in black denims
And strong cheap cologne
You one beautiful lie
Placed in a distant city
Between oceans and seas
You are one beautiful lie
Around my heart
And around my skin

Too potent to hide.

THE ONE

He insists on holding me
all night like am going to fall off
Cause he overheard from my friends that
that the kind of love I wish for,
He insists on morning kisses and giving me his
peaceful chest to lie on,
For he knows he's my calm,
He climbs on my window
 Cause I still live with my
parents and he can't
wait to see me the following morning,
He never mentions beauty
He calls me the stars
he loves evenings when my
Guard are by the fireplace,
and there's nothing on me,
I don't know what to do with
the days where am not beside him,
Am dull like the Skies
when it's about to rain,
I smell like tears.

UNFORGETABLE NIGHT

That night I
I left my door ajar,
So that if you showed up
you would just come in easily
and tell me sorry you were late,
Then we would make up,
share some more night memories
and fall asleep together,
Two decades later and I
still leave an inch open
for some air before 3am
when thoughts of you
trot in...
And I can't breathe.

WRONG TURN

 I remember our lips bruising
against each other... And the tip of
your nose sweating around mine,
I remember our arms slightly
touching and some words guiding us home,
Then I remember why you were here,
You were just reminder
that life has love in it, Like a road sign,
Turn left, turn right! With you I turned left,
And I keep going back and forth to read again,
I took the wrong turn,
But I drive there ,again and again,
Just to be sure, I read the sign, I forgot the other way,
Where there's no You or we,
Where paths are undeniably chaotic and know only of love.

LIKE THEY ALL DO

I almost loved you...
Then one morning you
 turned by the window,
And drew all the curtains,
Like they all do...
You let this morning see me
bare,
I almost loved you...
Then you smiled back at me, like they all do...
A smile which deceived my
heart into believing that it will last.
I almost loved you...
Then a memory of him crossed my mind,
Like they all do,
Then I ran for my life without looking back,
I almost loved you,
Just almost.

TELL ME

Tell me that love doesn't scare you
So I can run my fingers deep
Where its fetched and stuck to the heart,
Tell me am that dream Keeping you awake,
And I will stay up with you
So we can tame those tinkles and butterflies
And make stars our own
Tell me you love me again and
I will rewrite our kisses and breathes
Into countable love notes
Starting here and touching forever's
For baby I do not love little But wild,
And I do not run at all
Lest am running at the rate of heartbeats
Inside of your mind,
Just tell me.

LEAVING THIS TOWN

I heard that you left town,
With the bag I gave you,
Bragging it was D&G's

I heard that you left town, In my sandals
Stepping on everyone's feet.

I heard that you left town
With the tickets I bought for us,
Bragging you will never come again.
I heard that you left town, In my jacket,
Taking compliments from every stranger your way.
 I heard that you left town,
With my heart
Bragging of how
There was nothing left between us.

SEASONS

The winter rain has poured quicker than
last time, autumn leaves
have fallen without the hesitant of time!
 The spring dust has settled
And those summer burns are fading
under the skin miraculously,
But you…..you still hate the sound of my voice!
You still fall so far away from my pleas,
We can be seasons you know? Falling, settling,
fading and pouring
Into each other's dreams, without changing who we are,
Or the things we say to each other now that we no longer speak.

FAMILY

We look like each other, we wear the same silk clothes,
on our departure God shoved the best of clays
from a beautiful valley, slit it to pieces breathed into us at once.
He send us down here to lay in one skin,
(our mothers belly)! We are each other's spring,
we bounced out as joys, crying so they could smile,
to each one of us we should keep
an eye, a heart, a smile, our everything.

EACH SEASON

He was FIRE...
always looking to burn
everything HIS way,
I was the SEA...
good enough to pacify his FLAMES,
and drown him in
VAST enough to be left
behind
when WINTER came.
It was that seasonal.

FRIDAYS

You told me Fridays are for fools and I told
You they are for everyone!
Some would drink and party their souls away,
For they have had enough of the week,
Others lived it just like the rest of their days and
Those were the lucky ones!
This Friday I sit here drinking to forget you,
And I don't know, I feel like a fool,
And somehow lucky that I get to talk with the
bartender, told him you were never the whiskey type
he agrees !
You were a terrible love to love.

HOPELESS ROMANTICS

What's with hopeless romantics? They're often
Left on love sights, mourning, loving still and aching!
And that mess of a heart still gets back out, shining,
Still tender and kind,
Then it begins to wander, for another, for a chance
In eternal, without shame, without bitterness,
They are like givers of love, the gods and the goddesses,
Those hearts form a new despite the brokenness,
They reform and they are ready to give,
hopeless romantics are immortal.

LOVE HAS NO SECRET

If love only knew the taste of coffee on frosty mornings
He would be mine,
If love knew the songs, the rhythms, the sounds…
He would be next to me right now,
If love knew the emptiness, the aches, the places,
My heart would be his home,
But love tends to quiet every time there's noise,
Gets misunderstood every time it speaks,
Becomes everything, becomes something,
becomes nothing, love is a thing with no secrets.

MY BELOVED

The night is worn out, weary and torn it sank down
With your thoughts,
I couldn't wait to erase the sadness in your skin,
And wear it into the day,
Imagine what I would do to you,
Think, beloved,
When your tears are but the quench to my thirst,
I will bathe in that reverie,
When your joys are the falling buds in that
Tulip of a heart,
I will gift my charms so when you laugh
You laugh longer than it originally lasts,
When your mind wanders into warries
I will stitch memories into dreamcatchers place them
Upon Your head, Think my love,
The sun rising so your heart can beat next to mine,
Imagine what I would do to you,
I would ask the universe to tilt whenever we part,
So we slide back together uniformly,
 And while you live wherever your dreams are,
There I will send the magic of the sky
So your eyes may glow,
So much like you, upon my heart.

LOVE'S WORK

Love's not meant to make you feel better,
Neither does it make you feel wanted!
Anything can make you do that,
Love is meant to break you
Then meant you again,
Then break you once more,
And it stays,
Nothing moves it away,
It reigns inside of your heart for generations,
Love only urges you to give even thou,
You will never get anything in return.

FOREVERS

Some forever's have a name,
Some sad,
Some happy,
Some impossible,
Some forever's have a name,
 And mine's you.

MAGICAL MORNING KISS

He made it clear before this morning kiss,
"put this in your poetry…am not going
 to be part of a stanza where
you cry, where you praise me for leaving,
 am staying and this will be lifetimes!
Then he planted a kiss to seal that
His magical kiss is the fountain outside our castle,
What a kingdom!

DO NOT SETTLE

Do not settle, be the wind,
Brush their hair gently with your silent halloos,
Appear like the moon on dark nights,
Do not run, be still,
So everyone dances to the tune in your heart,
Die if you have to,
We can bury all that beauty but not
The scars upon your bones.

THE FOOLS

To think that the world would end
And I would be next to you,
To find these thoughts comforting is foolish,
What's death without
your scent? What's life without you?
What words would bring you back?
To think that you think of me
and to hold those thoughts hostage
To think that you will be mine,
Is foolish!
What's beauty without it's beast?
What's love without the other?
What's happiness without a laugh?
To wait here in silence
And to think that you would hear
To be dear to those thoughts, Is foolish!
What's you without that magic?
What's me without you?
What are poems with a
muse you will never see?

THE TRUTH ABOUT YOU

I want to tell you the truth tonight,
I want to put my heart in the oven,
And we will look together how
baked it becomes on certain degrees,
we might eat it afterwards for its gentle and soft!
I want us to be friends,
So when I tell you we will love, cry and laugh,
And that you won't forget! I want to tell you the truth,
I want to look in the mirror
and pull my eyes out slowly and fast,
So you can wear them! And we will look together how
darker it becomes when we cannot breathe,
Then I will tell you the truth....
You are beautiful, You are perfect,
You can do it, You are success, You are love,
You are so many good things.......
I want to tell you the truth....tonight,
Without feeling that it will be shattered
when those storms come,
I want to tell you the truth,
A truth you will never forget!
Please let me.

THE RIGHT TIME, THE RIGHT PERSON

I love to hold hands or lock them in
and squeeze tighter!!
And yes I know it's kind of babyish
gesture nowadays,

I love to be kissed right!!
maybe when we can't stand fit
cause we had too much to drink,
and we don't care who's watching!!

I love to be held when am still
cause that's how you tip the heart,

I love to be a stanza in someone's song
when I can't fit right,
Cause that's how homes are created.

Cause there's never the right person!
There's never the right time!
But there's a taste of love and eternity
in those little moments,
However short they last.

IT'S ALRIGHT

It's okay to say what you
want to say when you want to,
It's okay to smile even when no one smiles back,
It's okay to tell how you feel over and over again,
It's okay to be you... It's not okay to bury your
inner feelings at the bottom of your heart,
It's not okay to smile when you are sad,
It's not okay to say what you don't feel so you can fit,
It's not okay to be another
when you are so beautiful inside,
It's okay to be a mess,
It's not okay to love perfections for that's a
suit of armor for imperfections.

THE LORD'S GRACE

Have seen Lord on day I can't laugh,
With tears rolling down my eyes much faster
than the pain in my heart, But Lord said nothing,
He sat there and while I poured my troubles He listened,
Have seen Lord on days when I had nothing at all
and He said "this you have is enough"
But I wanted more and I told Him this is not
what you created me to settle for!
But He still listened, And I think He smiles
and says "I created you child and am the giver and taker"
Have seen Lord on darker days, when I couldn't see a thing,
He was there reminding me of things which didn't
need to be seen but felt, And he asked me to stay,
I see the Lord each second of my life,
He's here He will always be here.

UNBELIEVABLE

I cannot believe they said you are heavy,
But in my arms you feel more a lot like home...
I cannot believe they said it was never the right
time,
With me right now time has stopped, and we
have designed it into moments,
I cannot believe they said you are not enough
I don't seem to want
anything more whenever I look in your eyes...
I cannot believe they left you to shatter...
I can never find a way out of this place of ours
where our love blossoms.. I cannot believe they broke
you...
Such tender being, So firm and beautiful,
I cannot believe they never loved you...
you... You my love are made
of fragments and little forever's
vowed together as eternal love,
I cannot believe they blind themselves to your
tears,
I can't stop looking and wiping them away...

THE MOON AND I

Am like the moon
and it's delight,
A little bit mad
about the sun!
A little friendly with
the stars,
And when I can't shine
I come split in halves
or tangled in phases!
And when I shine
Am no longer empty
just full and beautiful.

BY THE SEA

I would love to stay by the sea, A little bit longer
So I can familiarize myself
with the tides and the sound which never end...

I would love to stay by the sea while am still young,
Because now my heart cannot listen
carefully to the wind which sways it away,
It still would beat with no wisdom of love...

I would love to stay by the sea a little bit longer,
When I can still make wrong choices,
For when the waves approach the sand, I still ran away and giggle...

I would love to stay by the sea, A little bit longer
If you stay with me,
So you lock my your arms on mine
So we can listen as it translates
what our hearts want with each other.

DAWNS AND DUSKS

Mornings are like silences,
A little bit cold and quiet! Unlike sunsets...
Full of goodbyes and endings, Love's like both...
Always warm in the middle,
until you reach out to the edge! or look back at the beginning,
But sometimes it's the heart,
Some withstand silences, Some know goodbyes,
Others are used to the cold,
But you my love are everything, you are the words
Yet you speak none,
You are the goodbye thou I never let go,
You make me a little bit cold to the universe,
Then warm me when thoughts of you kick in,
You empty me on these days you away,
And carry a piece of me wherever you go!
Isn't that beautiful...?
Your absence and presence are like dawns and dusks,
So beautiful and fascinating.

THE LAST TIME WE SPOKE

The last time we spoke I wanted to tell you to meet
Me there, where we loved to sit
And do nothing,
But I thought to myself, I will tell you tomorrow,
Days have gone by,
Time has tried its best to make me forget,
People have tried to make me remember,
The last time we spoke,
I was sure we will never end, But we did,
And sometimes I feel like am running
Out of time, I need to tell you this
I still think of you.

SHAME THEM

Shame those who are stingy with their hearts!
While they feast on others love,
give a piece of yourself and not
do no ask like they do
for another piece in return.

WHO'S SILLIER...?

Tell me why I loved wrong, why I thought you were like this sun by day and the stars by night, but you are nothing like them, tell me why I still cry or stay up with your name at the back of my head, and you, You are not the one! Tell me why you mean so much yet am nothing to you, who amongst us is much sillier,
The one who left right after we drowned or the one who still thinks of the other, but to tell you the truth it's never a ending story, things don't break like that, and loves darling loves don't leave like you did.

WHAT HAVE WE BECOME?

If I loved you this way,
Without reason,
Without sight of what's left now,
What would we have become?
If I can remember These places
And the mornings
You fetched my coat with my coffee
Where would we be my love?
If I could breathe this way,
just by the thought of your
hands sliding past my neck,
wants so despicable
And the Shameless longings
What would we be my love?
What would we be?

WE NEVER LAST

We are like rainbows
Hunting down quenching
spots when it freezes.
We are that beauty in seconds
Admired and taken photos of,
Seen only when cold
curls us to the inside
And a calm sun peeking through
soothing the skin, we do not last
We were meant to be the story,
The fairy tale,
With happy beginnings and unknown ending.

IF YOU WERE HERE

If you were here with me my love,
These soft tears would fall on your chest,
If you were here with me my love,
These dry lips of mine
would tremble between your own,
If you were here with me my love
These thoughts of you would be supplicated
into stars under this sky I watch,
If you were here with me my love
In this darkness I know my love
You would lead us home but my love
Two decades are gone by and the typewriter
which wrote our first story
lies in silence between our hearts.

MY DECEMBER MOON

You are my December moon,
I love to sit here and talk to you,
I fall asleep under your light, You are the stars…
Before you left you told me wild stories
Of the skies,
Then you promised to climb there first
So you can watch over me,
I watch you up there too,
Even on sunny shining days,
This I will never forget that you are never
Truly gone.

PLAYING JANUARY

Am playing January this October like you
Played me, always writing my name
On falling winter leaves and letting my
Head burn on summer days,
Now I get it...
There's never the wrong season for love
Only a little colder after you left.

SALT

He reminds me of places I forgot,
The passionate kind,
Places with graffiti as truths,
Here love greets you with a cleared throat,
We pass time letting hands run around the
abandoned buildings, then we switch glances,
and once again he says am beautiful,
then we laugh so loud,
cause that's a lie and we both know it!
But when he says that my tears taste like salt,
I pause for he is right,
I cry because we won't play Queen and King long,
Or because the night is young and I can
Never go home with him.
All this truths brew salty tears.

ONCE MORE

Sing to me under the light of these stars
Before that fateful night catches up with us,
Tell me lies and I will listen closely
I will remember the moment
I will be ready to let go,
Wait for me at our favorite spot I will come
there and tell you the things we wish
to hear, Let's go back a bit,
Minutes after the fall, Let's listen,
Let's walk away from there
holding hands, laughing,
So that if you have to leave, I will never
have to look for you in these sentences
And there will be no storm between you and I,
From this moment on.

A WONDERFUL MUSE

You are the color in the skies when
Dark calms the evening with sighs and goodbyes
You are the fine alignment of stars
When I look up and I can't contain this
beauty,
You are the night
between my lit candles
You are everything yet nothing at all!
You will never be mine but you belong
to me,
You are the shape of this heart before
It's death...
You are the pain which makes my heart beat
slowly, faster and then never at all.

FORGETTING YOU

Your name popped up in my keyboard
today while I was typing lies of how I
forgot about you,
Then it hit me!
I still remember you! Even after listening to
these songs which teach us how to forget
Even after tearing my diary
away, where I wrote everything
about you,
Have read poetries too urging me to let go
I was sure I had healed,
Because I smiled immensely
I didn't think of you anymore,
But now here we are again
am trying to remember how I almost forgot,
And you!!! You don't even know
That right now am aching for you.

REMIND ME

If I ever seem to forget
those soft bumps and the love hues!
Look for me under the
the light of the morning sun,
I can't shine bright!
Am in between the night am the dawns,
If I forget to love
Remember that one day
I couldn't close my eyes because you were
right here!
If there comes a time when life snatches
The curves, The soft tides The long kisses
And the stars in the skies,
The poetries,
Come back to me with the same arms
where I lay,
Remind me...

YOU SHOULD SEE THE MOON

You should see the moon right now,
 wrestling the clouds! And keeping on its feet,
 chasing the stars, making colors around it
like it knows it's being watched,
it looks beautiful, is that how it breathes?

LOVE & LEAVE

It's nothing to love and to be left,
as it is to love and not to be loved,
I wonder which one I pick from your
Absence, did you just leave, or did you
Just not love me as I loved you?
I'll feel all these feelings altogether,
to be left and not to be loved.

ME AND YOU

You are like me
we breathe, we bathe,
am like you, I love, I laugh.

But we are different,
for when you forgot me
and I still remember all of you.

LET ME CATCH YOUR TEARS

Tears will fall, not today, not now,
but when it rains, and I hope this time
a tornado of joy fills your empty.

And those unstoppable waterfalls
will carry your mascara down to the lips,
and this time there will be someone to
catch each drop.

HE STILL THINKS OF YOU

I love the night, the same way I love you,
this is where you love to hide,
you and your secrets,
it's beautiful to see you here like this,
helpless, unaware,
thinking you won with your silence
but you spoke to me time to time
you told me nothing and I understood,
I earned those quiet whispers…

'he still thinks of you too'

YOU WILL FIND LOVE

You will find love, someday,
doesn't matter how, but you will never
have to ask when to kiss their lips,
you will never have to ask when to hold their
hands and lead them down the mountain
for an adventure,
you will find love someday and you will do
whatever you wish with them,
and they will be happy.

KEEP RISING

You are broken but alive,
you are beautiful but alive,
you are sick but alive,
you are weary but alive,
 as long as you are alive,
you will have another day,
to fight,
to get better,
to be strong,
to be meant,
you are alive as many times,
in many forms, keep
 rising.

POETS RUN THE WORLD

Poets think they run the world,
well they do, the way they make you
cry! The way they leave you wanting,
the way they start those hidden wars
upon your heart,
the way your eyes close,
the way you twist yourselves while you walk
thinking that the world under your feet
trembles,
but they are not alone,
you make them feel too
and those things they will never write.

PLEASE LET ME

You should educate me, not my genitals
on how to take pains and nurse deep cuts,
you should love me,
not marry me off to the man
the age of my father so, he can love me for you!
you should help me sleep so I can dream
not send me to burn under this sun to get water
and feed the cattle which remind me of
the only sister I had,
am I not beautiful to you?
We don't have much but you we can fight,
Maybe together if you let me,
Am in fear you know, and I can't flee now,
Is it too late to ask you to let
Me grow at the middle of this nothing
Cause this way I will die
Beside my dreams, beside my home
Untouched..
Will you help me believe that there's
something more for me,
this is all I ask however little please let me.

LOVE AT MY DOOR

I know love will bring its unsteady pace
at my door, he wouldn't know what to say so
I can let him in, "sorry am late?" I think not! That
will sound like something he says all the time only
to get me changing my locks,
"may I come in?" no not that!
That will be too polite and obvious,
he will kick the door open
and assume his favorite place in the living room,
so that our conversation won't start with
why's but you should fix that right away,
he will then find a metal to make a steady door
so that we can chase each other forever
without wandering far,
I do not know whether I will love again,
but am keeping these bones straight so I can ran
fast across the rooms and hide,
I cannot let love settle,
It will tire, it will give up,
it will have to learn and catch up.

THE SAME PAIN

I wished you away today in the back of my
thoughts, I asked God to give you the same
intensity of pain! Or even more,
you should feel your heart shatter any moment from now
tearing those rib cages escaping just for some air,
you will run to scream it away in the stream
and your lungs will collapse, every bone in your
body will ask to split from the other
and this will go on and on,
long enough for you to call it a friend!
Long enough for you to get to the edge where
life and death draw lines,
then you will find me there, and beg me to end it!
In turn I will beg you to erase yourself from
my heart,
I know only then we will work together and
save each other.

WOULD YOU LOVE ME

Would you love me, if I were curved with bends and alleys?
Would you love me, without my pennies and jewels?
Would you love me, if I were the thirst upon your throat?
Would you love me, without my masks and flesh?
Would you love me, If I were invisible and pricked?
Would you love me, without my love and its returns?
Would you love me, if I were in a cage and you its freedom?
Would you love me, without my name and my eyes?

Would you?
Would you?

AM HIS

Girls stuck to champagne, men to scotch!
but my hands found their way around his
glass,
cause I knew how he liked his women,
rebellious, daring and more thirsty,
I no longer wake up between broken
unfinished wine bottles,
am on the front porch
where I can be what I want,
And am his.

PROMISES

Have loved, Yes I know,
To uncountable winters,
Then to unbearable summer
But first fall have seen the best,
In his blue eyes till it was warm again
Have loved yes I know,
From this edge to another through this universe
In Mauritius it was the best
Just lying and calling
Taking photos of each other
Till we came home at last
Have loved, this I know
A couple of lives and more,
Deaths too soon in tranquil
And in my last life I found him
A forever full of worth.

ENDLESS LOVE

And I see us laughing behind a delightful shadow
Laughter bringing us closer
Then your hand to my hip
And our laughter's crash into soft giggles,
Your left holds half of me
My left holds haven of you Our right locked together
A magic we never created A magic which created us,
A kiss and another
You humming away my life
And dancing together by the moon I see us my love,
Playing by the sea, running after the waves,
Never wanting the day to end, never wanting the
The night to end,
Then we fall all again each day in a scrambled rough work of
Unfinished chapters dying together holding hands
to run around in the next life.

HIS ROYAL MAJESTY

He ate me up like Amyotrophic lateral sclerosis,
Along my vertebrae's,
Every time he squeezed me between himself
I screamed,
But I wanted more of him like Chupacabra,
He liked my desperation!
His royal majesty was bleary.

He exhaled me into fumes and ashes,
Every time he puffed I vanished into thin air!
But inside me he consumed like my favorite drug,
His royal majesty cardiovascated.

He surfed me like a very dangerous wave, Along the pacific,
Every time he fell I seized like a pacifier,
But I wanted to be his favorite wave,
He avoided my drowning desire,
His royal majesty was mundane.

He drank me like boiled Cinchona bark,
Spitting me with disgust thou!
Every time I fell his soles were ready to crush me,
But I wanted him like a punch of cocktail,
He liked where I was kept for ages in a rusted glass!
His royal majesty was cosset.

He sang to me like "oh by the sweet"
 When I was gone, But I wanted to rise from the dead,
 his eulogy so flattering, His tears so convincing,
Onwards on his thrown he would rule, His royal majesty was lone.

IF YOU LEAVE

If you leave,
Leave my pieces scattered,
Scattered so I can pick each one of them,
Each one of them so I can remember,
Remember how it felt when it broke.
If you leave,
Leave with your map on,
On to where you go,
Go so I can stagger,
Stagger to find my own way again.
If you leave,
Leave and don't look back,
Back at what you left,
Left so I can love again.
If you leave,
Leave and never come back,
Back to break me again,
Again to find me gone,
Gone to a new story.

BARBADOS

"Have you seen the world?" She asks and almost breaking…
"what?" I ask conquering her innocence, But I heard each word!
"have you seen the world?" she asks again
This time I see those words escape her eyes And set free like smoke,
"yes have been to places" I nod looking away.
"how does it feel to be away from home?, how
Do those places look like? Are the lands filled with still
Dust like here, or is it ice like in some school books,
Is it all rock like some places in my geography classes,
What are people like? Are they nice like aunt
Georgina or mean like uncle timothy?
What food do they eat? Do they speak our language?
Are they happy or sad most of the times like grandpa…
How about their puppies are they lovely Like Texas…
She goes on and on with questions so excited for an Answer
"tell me tell me"
But how do I tell this little four year old
About all these places, the universe, homes and all its chaos
Without tearing her apart or sounding insane…

"one day I will take you to Barbados there's a lonely wild
Surf in the Eastern coast, then there you can dine with
The stars"

THE ONE SHE LOVED

With great unsatisfactory she looked beyond,
for the man she loved hugging the man she married tightly,
how could he not stand at and claim her?
She wondered!
Haven't she been enough?
The priest announced its time for a kiss,
she wet her lips and smiled,
she looked everywhere for the one she loved,
between the glooms, cameramen and the elderly,
he wasn't anywhere,
she observed the one she married
and sure she thought she belonged there not!
Her eternity was with who she loved,
who never turned on any of her occasions!
The chariots were ready to take them away,
she clearly looked close at their rider
and sure he wasn't him she loved either,
she smiled to whom she had married and they rode happily,
beyond the mountains below the rivers,
on seas and every city they travelled,
she couldn't erase the memory of him
who she loved,
deep in the night she searched never giving up,
sometimes she would murmur in her lost,
"Where are you?"
He who she had married would answer,
"Am right here"
She wet her lips and smiled for him.

LOVE WILL KILL YOU

A heave of sadness has fallen upon my eyes,
I can cry but I cannot see,
I feel alive yet dead to you,
I can smile while my heart breaks,
I cannot believe one person can love another this way
despite the warnings written in bold
on their skin,
"love will kill you so why drink on?"

DO YOU FEEL IT?

Do you feel it?
the echo of the hollow in your chest when you talk?
The loneliness spilling while you walk and it rolls
It self in red carpet then folds so you can sit,
Do you feel it?
The breaking before 3am which leaves dreams leaking
to nightmares, waking to scars, living in the memories,
the love which can never be received asking where else
it can serve this way,
do you really feel it?

SUICIDE

I am a woman who rolled into bed today at 10:00 pm
Aware of a 3:00 am scenario, I would have chose
To choke myself to sleep and close that window,
But we met again like last night, my basket empty
So ready to fetch so much poems so you can read,
Cause all those 3:00 am trains carry such treasures.
I am a woman well read, beige and have
 eaten so this body is chubby
 enough to bury the filth in your hands when
those thoughts you have of me trot in and
you see nothing more than your pleasure,
and don't forget all you say
 about my fat will never get to my bones,
I am a woman calm enough to forgive resurrect and become,
Because you buried me beneath words forgetting that am gifted
Have rearranged each and brought them
 up with their positives, Hate for the love, You can't for you will,
Nothing for everything, Cursed for hope,
Useless for useful, And you are not for I am.
I am a woman eyes wide open, heart tightly
shut and mind glowing with all this beauty,
Have made sure this will be hard to find have put it on the inside
And sometimes I will wear my makeup just
to shock you, just so you can think about it
 like there's anything more beyond the mask.
I am a woman wiser with my silence, brilliant with my words,
I will tell you about the world, about places I want to go
but I will never reveal my homes my safe havens…
I am a woman a purse full of love, kindness and happiness,
I am a woman with well knight wings designed for every trial.
I am a woman not worried about the man
at the end because who was here first when I became,
I am a woman and when it rains I want to run wild,
When there's thunder I want to say hallo,
When there's lightning I wish for a strike I am a woman,
Mighty but fragile, Knowledgeable but curious, Fearless but afraid,
Bold but vulnerable I am a woman, a bit loud, a bit me

STAY

Every time I think of you
I wither,
I feel myself slowly turning and falling,
like pieces of withering petal
have been watered often and you
keep growing beneath my roots,
you are the most unwanted weed
only that I brought you here myself against
your will, the way you shake where I grow
trying to set yourself free, is the same way
I hold you firm beneath me and shout,
"stay am not ready to break, am not ready to un root"

A SONG OF LOVE WITH LAURA
(the southern belle poetics)

Have come close to the truth than I ever was
to love there's nothing breakable here,
and lies are fried and tied like in the last
scene of love, clear and unbearable!

Yet I see you and my heart still yearns.
I know this lesson yet I refuse to memorize it,
I am not a moth to your flame and the truth is
Closer to me now than love ever was. Burning me
Breaking this unbreakable heart.

Now look at me shattered and split into halves,
Some meant to watch you forget, others lost in
Your silence, is it any comfort to say the truth
Brought me close home than you ever did.

Home for me was you! And it is home no more,
My vagrant heart wanders now, searching for
The self that have lost loving you…

IF TIME COULD...

Time doesn't fly where I come from, it doesn't talk,
thou it has had enough laments, prayers, curses of the universe!
So it leaves us with more time to love,
To grieve, to live, to remember, to forget to become, un become
Time gives itself back.

THE PREACHER
A poem with Parka

The preacher rants and chants walking the
lonesome street of salvation! Blabbing and spitting
from between his gum,
booting the neighborhood awake,
from within his lungs, with a
dying megaphone of 2000 years ago,
he is coming, he will come, he's here!
and you will never know.
He parades halleluiahs where children have been playing
all day long,
breathing verses all over the Bible
except from songs of Solomon,
"the world is ending, the blood moon has caught
with us, it is the end of times" he says at the top of his voice,
that we hear his lungs collapse… the sun is setting happily in the
west,
"repent for darkness has found us awake again"
There's a grave silence afterwards,
The preacher rants and chants,
Walking in the lonesome streets of unfulfilled dreams.

ANOTHER SONG WITH YINA ROJAS

You were all I had,
All I could wish for and more,
Why you hurt me so bad,
And break what I adored?
Now all I have are images of what was,
Of what used to be,
A past I don't wish to look back,
But I must face my reality

Broken pieces I can't make of
Fading promises I can't comprehend,
Lost love I can never find
A tomorrow I am afraid to face
Without you.....

While I prepare on this journey
We both started taking another path,
Accepting and cursing I know for sure my heart
Will never have a place,
Without you....

For I can love you from afar,
Because together we can't play the part
Of tender lovers and best friends,
Just let me be without you, Let me see this to its end
Let me hold a forever around your soft palms
Let me forget the goodbye within a blink Let me be in that moment
Where we both longed for each other
And brought out sinful pleasures to the brink
Where our desires had no limit,
With a force that cannot be apprehended,
With a love that's unprecedented
With actions and Words that will forever live in the eternity
Of my heart and soul
Look, I am a dying soul Writing my wishes on the moon
When you can reach out and grasp my demons
But still my heart beats away and alone from you
Shouldn't our story be told in abyss and calm?
Or in forever and beyond? Or in every beat of your heart?
Just as we had promised before
Before the promises turned to lies,

Before they became more than flashing stars in the sky,
Before you told me how much you loved me
And before it all turned out to be a dream
What we had then what we have now
Uncommon and unpredicted Rising and falling
High and low knots
Why did we have to fall on this one weak notch?
What was stronger? Your ego, or our dearest love.......

DREAMY CICADA (1)

She is rising from the filth you bury her in,
that time you said she can't,
that time you said "look she will never rise"
after shaming her and retorting harshly upon her crown,
that time you looked on the outside and saw a broken
child who needed your pity,
that time you counted all you have done for her yet she
does nothing you said, that time you asked her for something
in return for she didn't deserve the world like the rest
of your kind,
that time you made her cut a piece of herself so she could fit,
all the times you hid her behind the curtains
cause it was abomination for her to exist then,
you buried her and she is rising, and this is not the end,
others cut from your clothe will come after you,
and she will still rise, she will still dream, she will soar,
billion times, nothing will bury her for long, she can never
stay down, she rises she will till the end of times.

DREAMY CICADA (2)

And all I could hear upon that moonless night
was the lyrical sound of a dreamy Cicada
I was half asleep,
Half awake,
Diffused into thoughts of you,
Reflecting,
Inflecting,
Deflecting,
Our Point of view,
Soo acute,
so obtuse,
so astute,
and you were over me,
above me, below me
and I was tripping,
falling, slipping, sliding
and finally drifting into peaceful
rhythmical sleep,
oh this dreamy cicada!
My
dreamy
cicada!

WRONG ABOUT MORNINGS

Maybe I was wrong about mornings I haven't
bathed yet, and am in my pajamas! there
are no coffee spots in Migwani so am tipping
Mbaluka for a large Delamere yoghurt,
The closest retail shop on my way to work,
Am chilling by the balcony in the office
I saw an old friend of mine and we had
A pleasant conversation and she invited me for
Tea cause she moved in the most beautiful
Mansion around, she is nice she's rushing to
teach schools just opened, I go about my business sipping
My vanilla pod Delamere yoghurt, and am not
Ashamed to hit play in my pc and keep Chris Brown
Playing, I will write more poems, and watch
Crazy rich Asians later, I hope to start work soon,
and have never been this happy to be alive in the
morning.

A LETTER FROM THE FUTURE

Things have changed a great deal here,
everyone has their own freedom slipped
inside their pockets like a treasure,
times faster here, one time you watching your
nephews and nieces cry to be tucked, the next
day they are trying to fight you for a television remote
to watch rated shows! A thing you will never understand
there are no Televisions there yet! I do not get it too.
its lazier here, I haven't gone out for the sun for days
but I can eat sleep well and pay taxes, you do not know what those
are too but I do not have much time to explain then later I will log
into social network and see people have never met celebrating their
madness, you wouldn't understand any of this, but you should see for
yourself, and since you can't you will be patient with me as I try to
get to the end.
 Love is little and people have
become louder, sadness visits often and it's evident,
there's little time for everyone, the sun feels closer,
the moon is far away, it even turned red a couple of months ago for a
night, do you think it was hungry with us?
women have turned the world around,
they can pray, they speak before men,
they have dreams, they can drive,
and they are barely home doing chores,
there are new types of music, new types of food,
new types of diseases, sometimes it feels like the end,

We communicate faster, not through letters
    Messengers or bonfires, but we
    lie more, and misunderstand easily,
    we slid smoothly into civilization,
    am writing from the future without a pen,
    am writing from the future with a heavy heart,
    I hope someone gets to read this letter
    I hope someone responds with a wiser heart,
                I hope someone understands,
        Life becomes tougher in

the inside and it happens faster in
the outside,
 Am writing from the future and I will forgive you,
  for starting this war,
  for ending it,
   for bringing it.

BEFORE THE END

Before the end I would love to be you,
I would love to be in those tender arms
welcoming mornings like Saturdays,
thanking the moon like a god,
praying for hearts like a nun,
but these words are not deaf,
and we all can see how well we fit,
without you breaking our hopes,
we are building what you crushed,
we shall rise time and again,
before the end, one will become,
everything you said they will never be.